Dr Gene Baillie

beyond the bottle

ve them will never thirst

illustrations by Ty Davis

n them a spring of water welling up to eternal life

The quoted ideas expressed in this book (but not Scripture verses) are not, in all cases, exact quotations, as some have been edited for clarity and brevity. In all cases, the author has attempted to maintain the speaker's original intent. In some cases, quoted material for this book was obtained from secondary sources, primarily print media. While every effort was made to ensure the accuracy of these sources, the accuracy cannot be guaranteed.

Unless noted otherwise, Scripture quotations are from the Holy Bible, English Standard Version (ESV), copyright © 2001 by Crossway Bibles, a publishing ministry of Good News Publishers. (This author capitalized the first letter of deity pronouns in ESV passages.) Scripture quotations marked NASB are from the New American Standard Bible,® copyright © 1960, 1962, 1963, 1968, 1971, 1972, 1973, 1975, 1977, 1995 by the Lockman Foundation, used by permission; NIV, the Holy Bible, New International Version,® copyright © 1973, 1978, 1984 International Bible Society, used by permission of Zondervan, all rights reserved.

Cover design and art by Ty Davis
Interior design and e-book by Will Malone

ISBN 978-0-9964972-5-1 (print)
ISBN 978-0-9964972-6-8 (e-book)

Printed in United States of America

Dr Gene Baillie

beyond

ive them will never thirst

the

bottle

illustrations by Ty Davis

n them a spring of water welling up to eternal life

I have been "bottled in" for 9 months.

This world is amazing now that I am out of the womb!

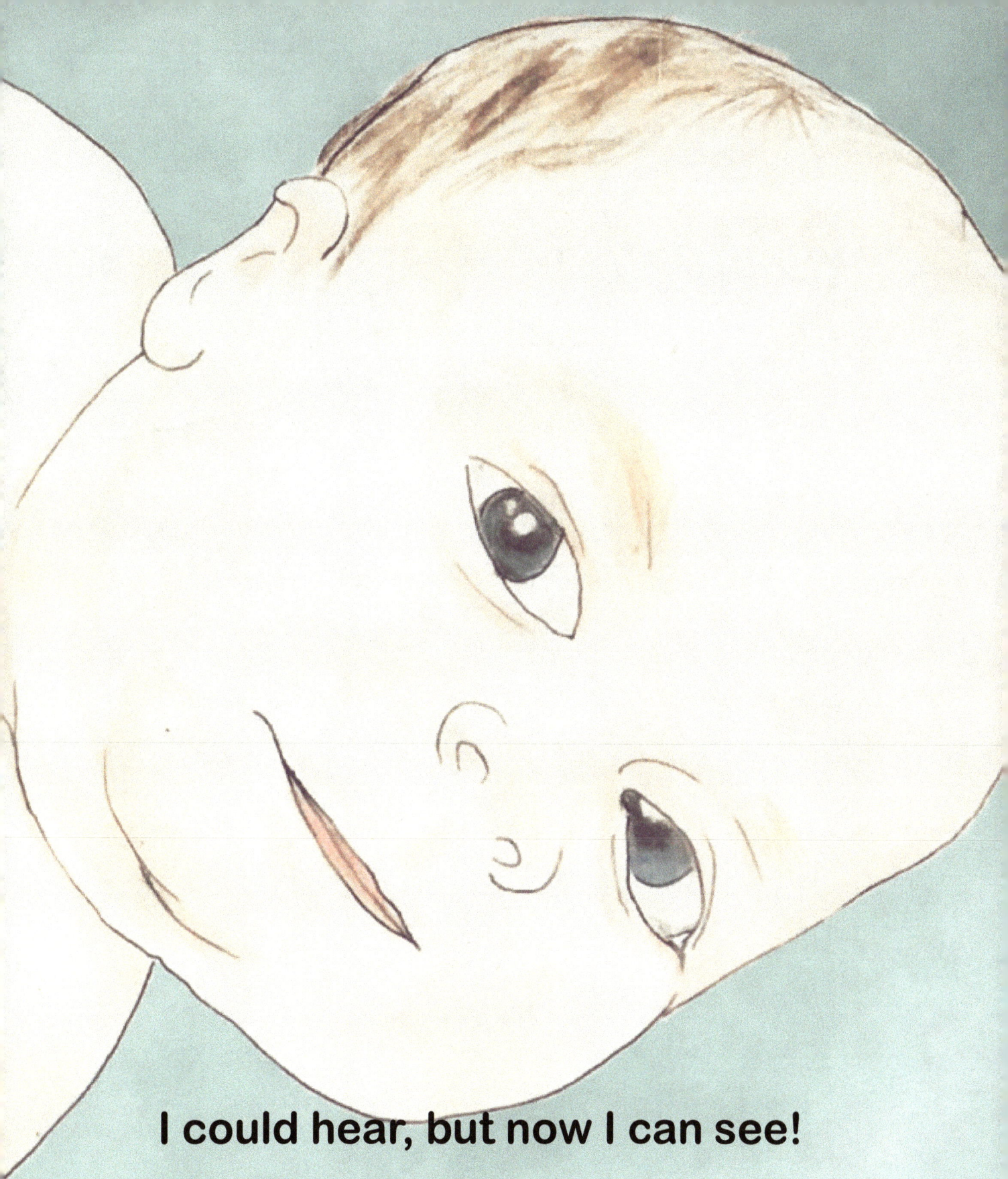

I could hear, but now I can see!

This milk tastes good, but I
wonder if there is something more...

This milk is good, but I am also missing the closeness to my mom and her milk.

I am curious

Anything else?

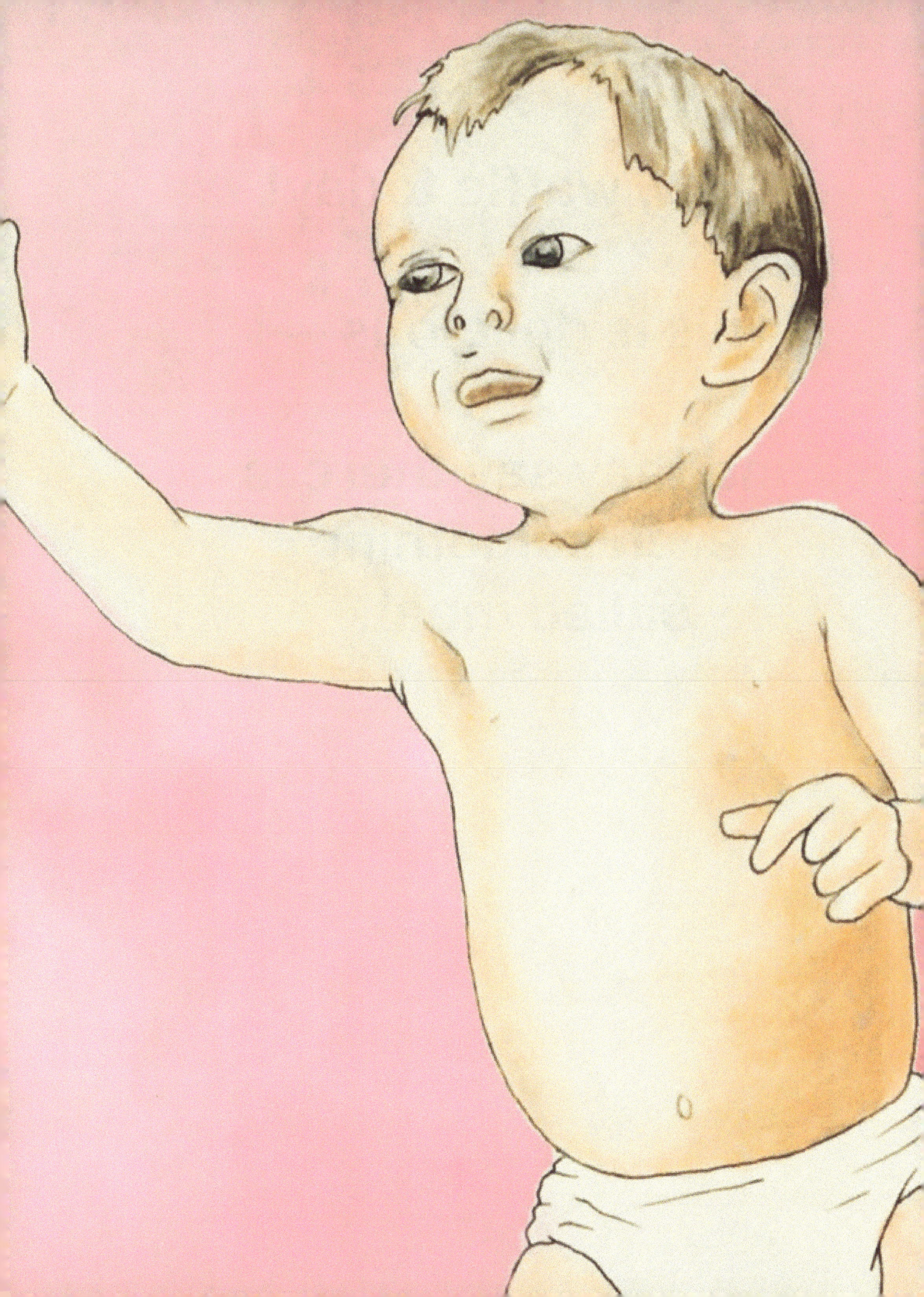

Wow, waffle today!

This is delicious —

and they say there is
even something
called meat.

Yes, this is so good, but I still want milk, so give me my bottle back!

I GAVE YOU MILK, NOT SOLID FOOD, FOR YOU WERE NOT YET READY FOR IT. INDEED, YOU ARE STILL NOT READY.

1 CORINTHIANS 3:2

This is a different kind of bottle with a different kind of drink. Tastes great! They say I am on a sugar high and the caffeine has me dancing. I am sure it is made from the purest ingredients and made just for me to enjoy.

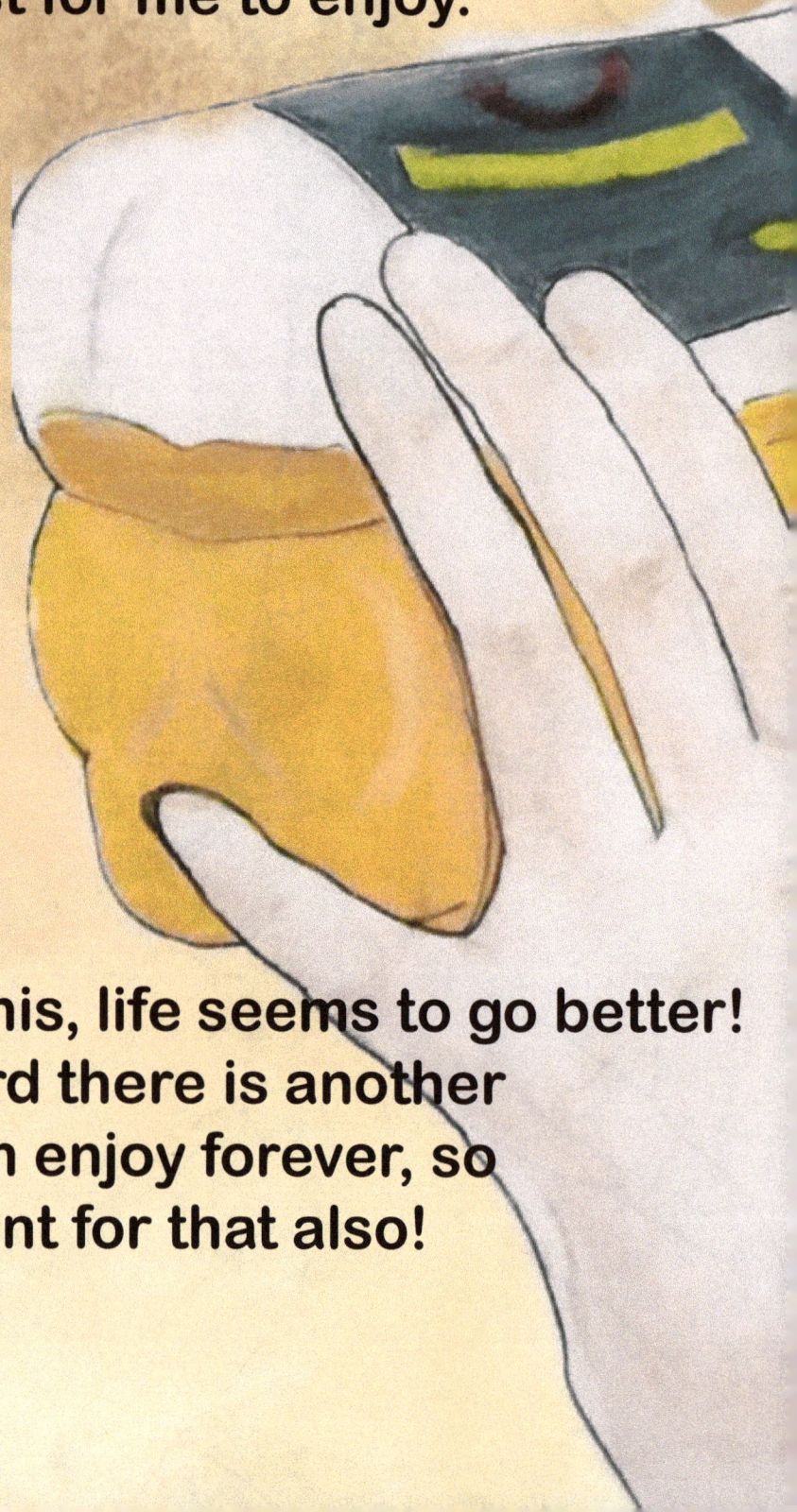

As long as I have this, life seems to go better! I also heard there is another drink I can enjoy forever, so I will hunt for that also!

They say this is next, but I have to wait until I am an adult, whatever that means.

I can only see dimly through this bottle, but once I drink it, they tell me there is a really, really fun life out there. When I observe people who drink too much from this bottle, I do hear laughter, but mostly I hear troubling things which don't make sense and are indistinct — even anger and arguing

Wow, I'm finally an adult and this bottle is amazing, but I keep having to drink more to get the same feeling.
It has a created date and says it is brewed from the finest of ingredients and the purest of water.
Someone said there is also a created date for me going back to the foundation of the world, whatever that means

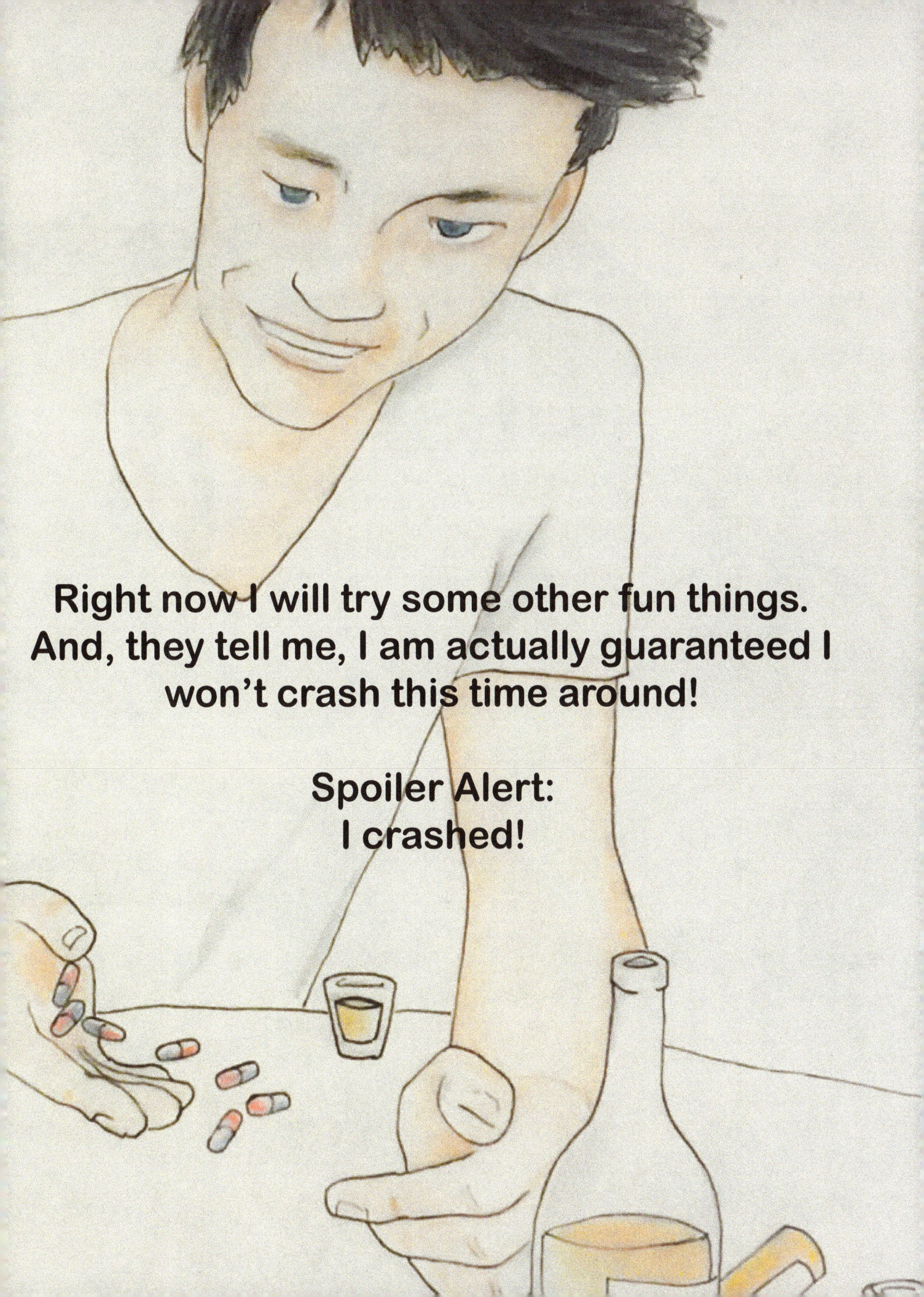

Right now I will try some other fun things.
And, they tell me, I am actually guaranteed I
won't crash this time around!

Spoiler Alert:
I crashed!

They told me to just try a couple more bottles and I did— but nothing changed. This is definitely not the good life I expected. I've tried draining several bottles and yet everything still is cloudy and fuzzy. This stinks! But I don't know how to get out of this cycle!

I just want to go back and start over, but I would look pretty silly drinking milk from a baby bottle

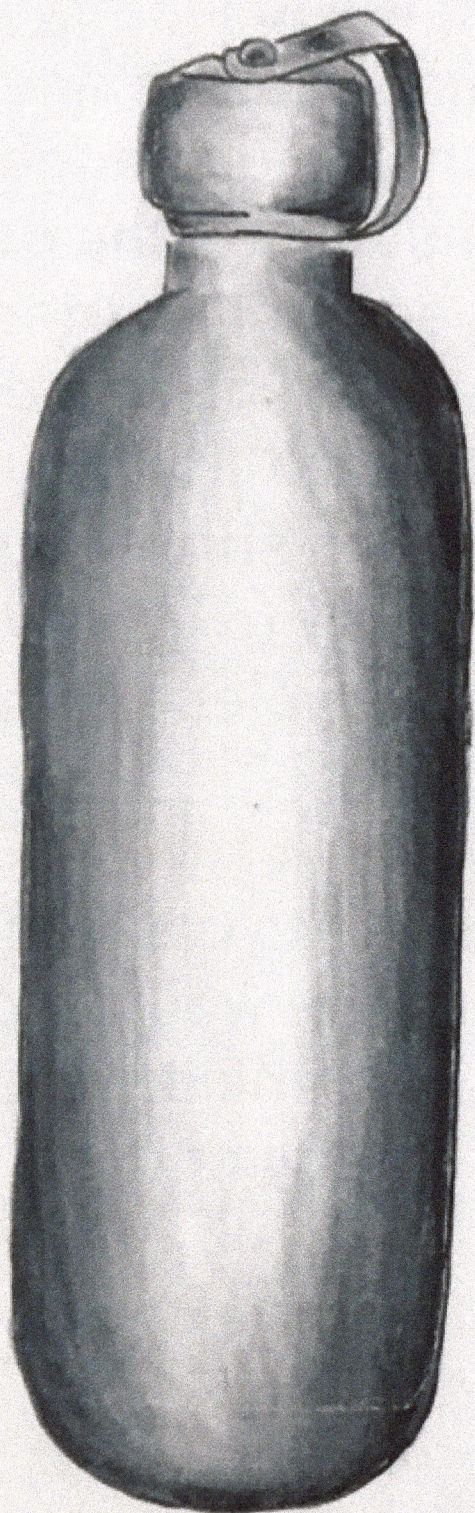

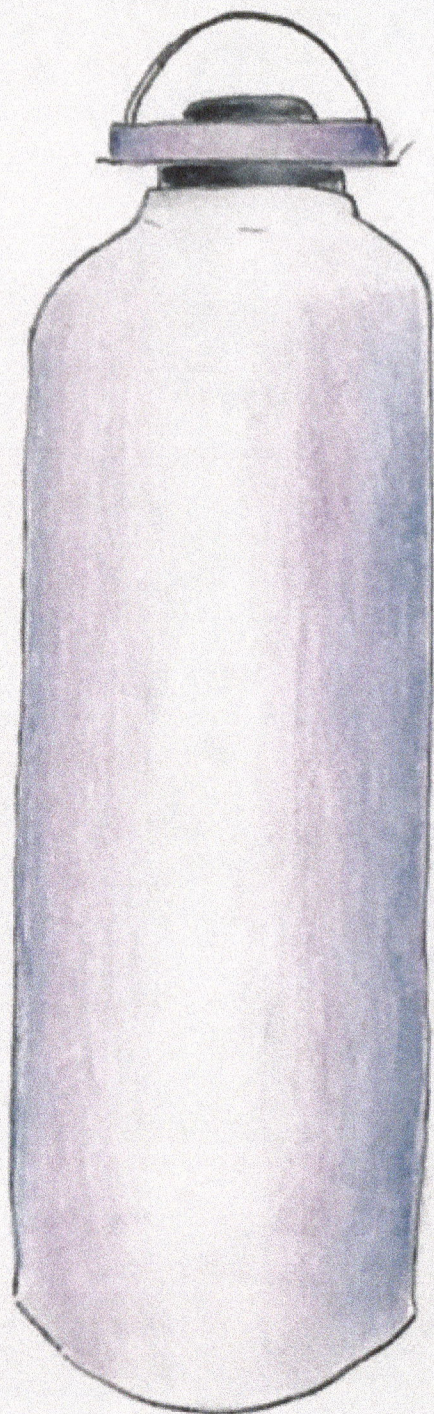

I am going to try going back to just water. But, no matter the bottle or contents, hot or cold, or what flavor I put in, this is just a form of water and I long for more! This never satisfies and is boring. I just get thirsty again

Someone told me there is living water that will satisfy thirst forever. Maybe I will look for that in the store

I have tried so many other things to satisfy. Fortune telling is definitely fake, and I haven't won the lottery yet.

Life seems like being on a deserted island, hoping someone will find my note in a bottle I dream of putting in the water, then someone coming to rescue me—I cannot do this myself!

I am reminded I inherited an old, old bottle my grandfather found on the shore of the Sea of Galilee many years ago. I did not try open it. I really want to know what the note inside says, but many wiser than I, told me it would lose its value. The cork is very brittle, and encrusted with barnacles. And, of course, I didn't want to break the bottle. I was told there is life beyond the bottle and to Google some clues, "Your Word have I hidden", "Your Word is truth", and "Open my eyes that I may see". I will pass the bottle and these clues along to my heirs and maybe they will figure it out

Sanctify them by the truth; your word is truth.

I can't seem to figure this life out, so I think I may just end it all. A gas tank is a big bottle, but it still is not the answer. I am at the end of my rope.

Nothing has changed!

No matter what I do, pills I take or bottles I drink, things do not get better!

Do not turn from the Lord to advice from fools, do not run after empty things that can not profit or deliver, for they are empty!

I am desperate for answers. I decided to follow advice to go to a church. The Pastor there sat down with me. He told me "I am" the problem!

And what I need is a 'Whom' beyond myself. As I listened about the Living Water and Spiritual Food, suddenly I felt a rustling within and understood — there is One who is the "I AM" answer to everything. He has come into my life and I will never be the same

How then will they call on Him to whom they have not believed? And how are they to believe in Him of whom they have never heard? And how are they to hear without someone teaching?… "How beautiful are the feet of those who bring the good news!"

Let me tell you about Jesus, God's Son, who came to earth and then died as a sacrifice for your sins, that you might have eternal life by faith and believing in Him, asking Him to be your Savior and Lord. Faith comes from hearing, and hearing through the word of Christ. Let's continue to meet together again to study more of His Word.

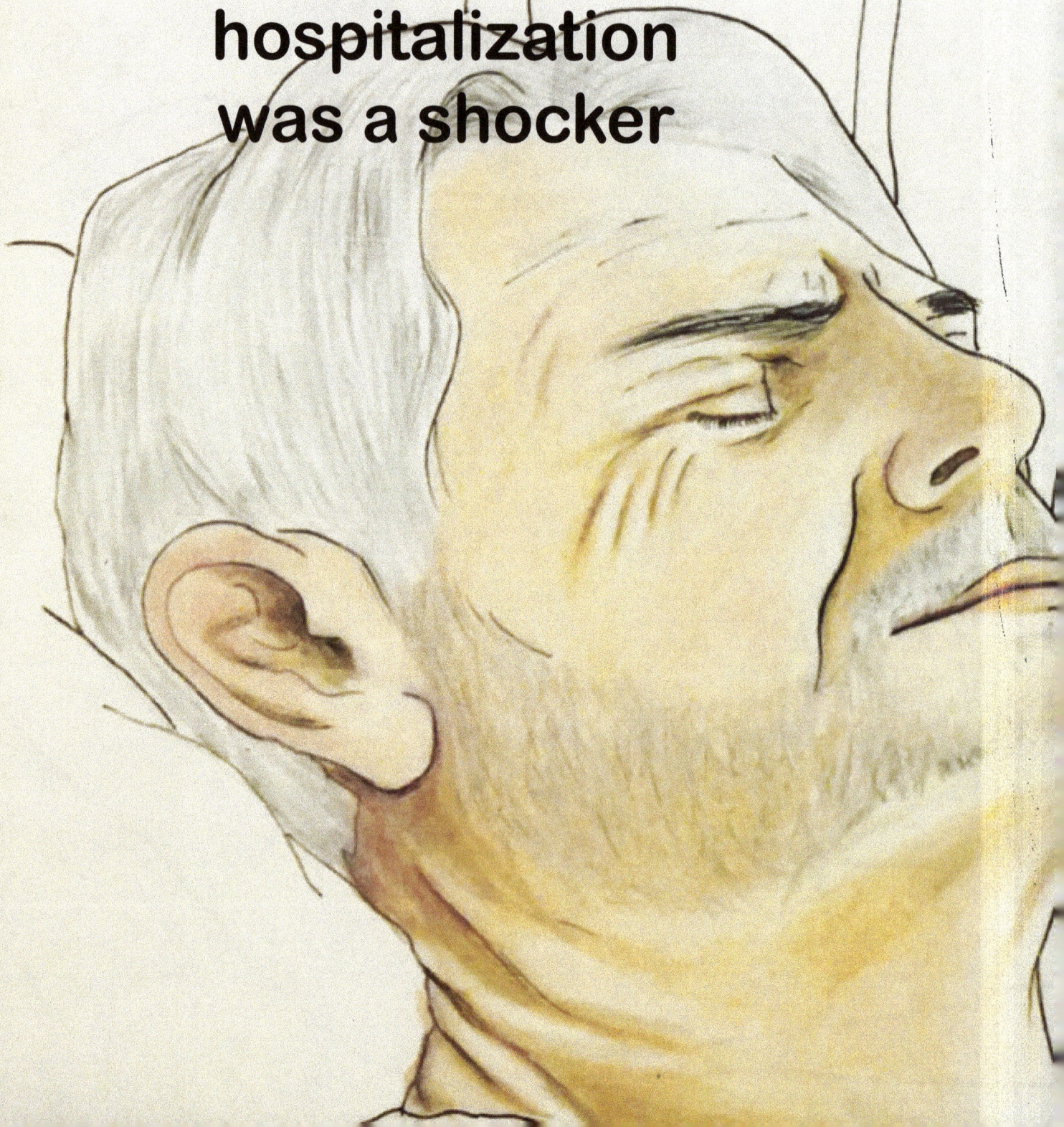

I was feeling better and doing well, then blindsided! This sickness and hospitalization was a shocker

I am told in former days these fluids were in real bottles. This is not my idea of the bottle I should have, but it is keeping me alive. I am told to have joy in trials and difficult circumstances, but I am not enjoying this at all!

CONSIDER IT PURE JOY, MY BROTHERS AND SISTERS, WHENEVER YOU FACE TRIALS OF MANY KINDS, BECAUSE YOU KNOW THAT THE TESTING OF YOUR FAITH PRODUCES PERSEVERANCE. LET PERSEVERANCE FINISH ITS WORK SO THAT YOU MAY BE MATURE AND COMPLETE, NOT LACKING ANYTHING. IF ANY OF YOU LACKS WISDOM, YOU SHOULD ASK GOD, WHO GIVES GENEROUSLY TO ALL WITHOUT FINDING FAULT, AND IT WILL BE GIVEN TO YOU. BUT WHEN YOU ASK, YOU MUST BELIEVE AND NOT DOUBT, BECAUSE THE ONE WHO DOUBTS IS LIKE A WAVE OF THE SEA, BLOWN AND TOSSED BY THE WIND.

JAMES 1: 2-6

What use is there if I die
without seeing the note in
the bottle! Another wise man told
me a buried treasure chest
needs to be opened to
reveal its treasure.
I have broken open the
bottle and the note says

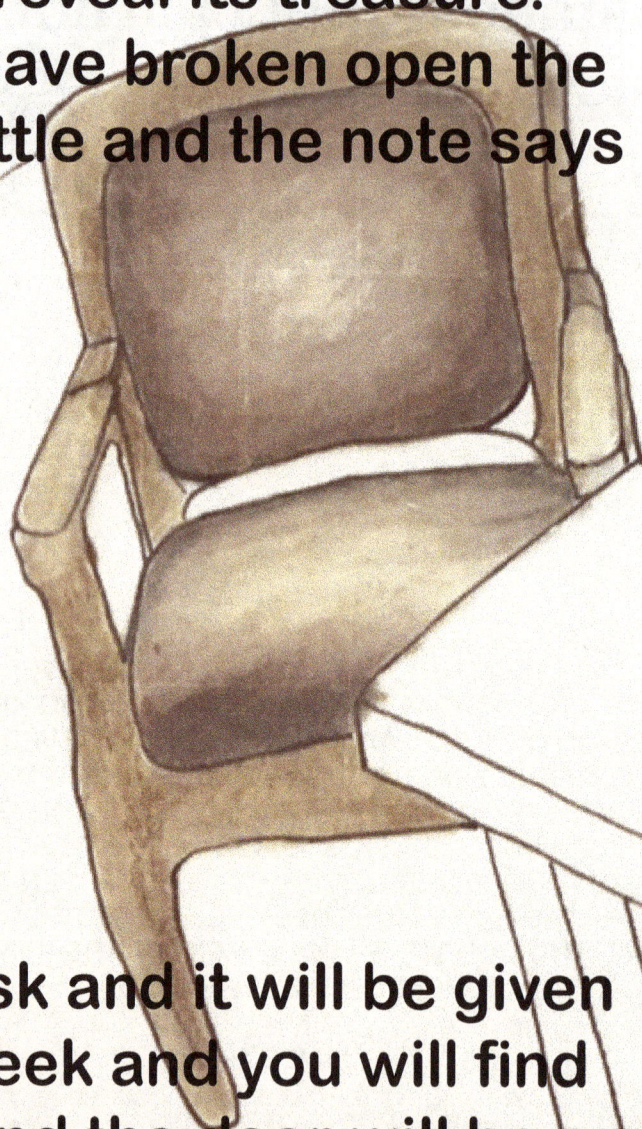

'Ask and it will be given
Seek and you will find
Knock and the door will be opened
Water eternal'
What does all this mean?

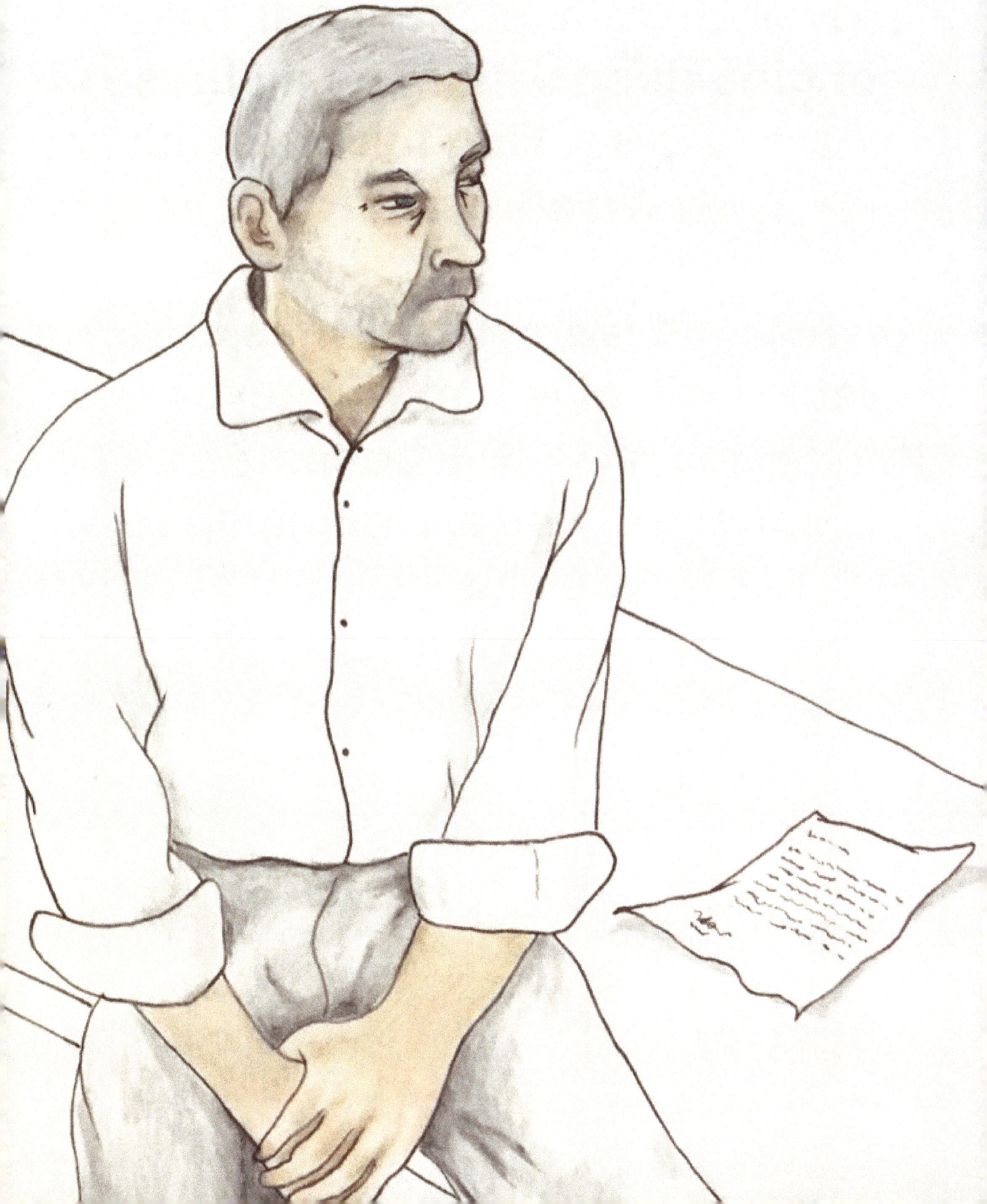

What a confirmation in that old bottle. Right now I know and feel everything has changed! That longing deep within me all these years was seeking for the drink I have now tasted.

Jesus said 'whoever drinks of the water I will give him will never be thirsty again— it will become in him a spring of water, welling up to eternal life'

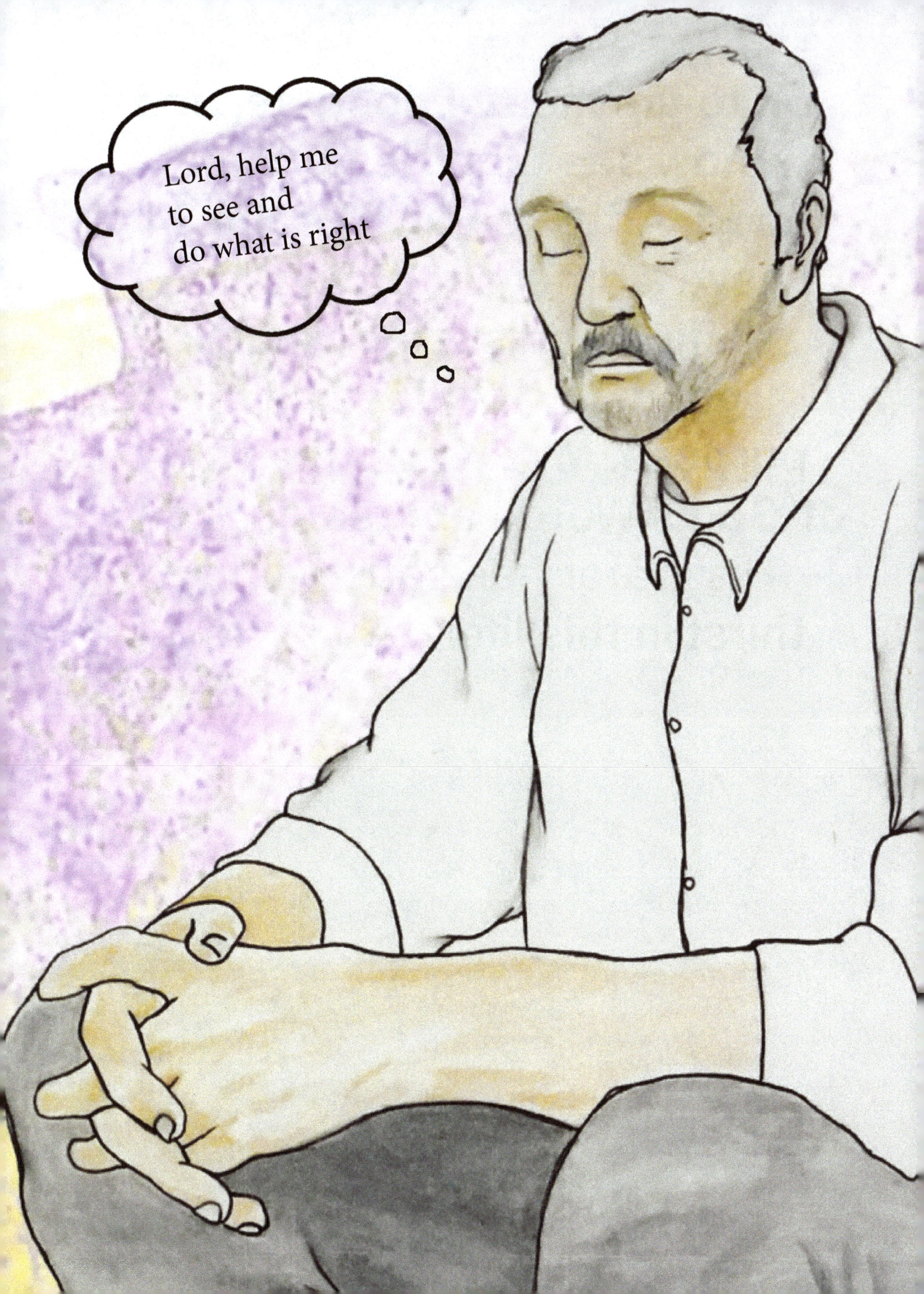
Lord, help me to see and do what is right

On to the meat! I do taste, and now see that the Lord is good. After reading Psalm 34 I have a different definition of tasting and seeing what is good. My life does have purpose. My meat is the truth of God's Word I am reading, and His Water has satisfied my thirst in this life and the next.

Here are all my tears in a bottle— those He promised to keep. It still makes for a cloudy view through the bottle of this life, but beyond the tears I perceive joy and mercy and know of the very pleasant place where I will dwell. I am at rest. I trust. I hope. I know. The best is yet to come, —beyond the bottle. 'Now in a mirror dimly, but then face to face!'

Even with its pain and difficulties, life is good. God is good and does good. He is preparing to take me home to enjoy Him forever!

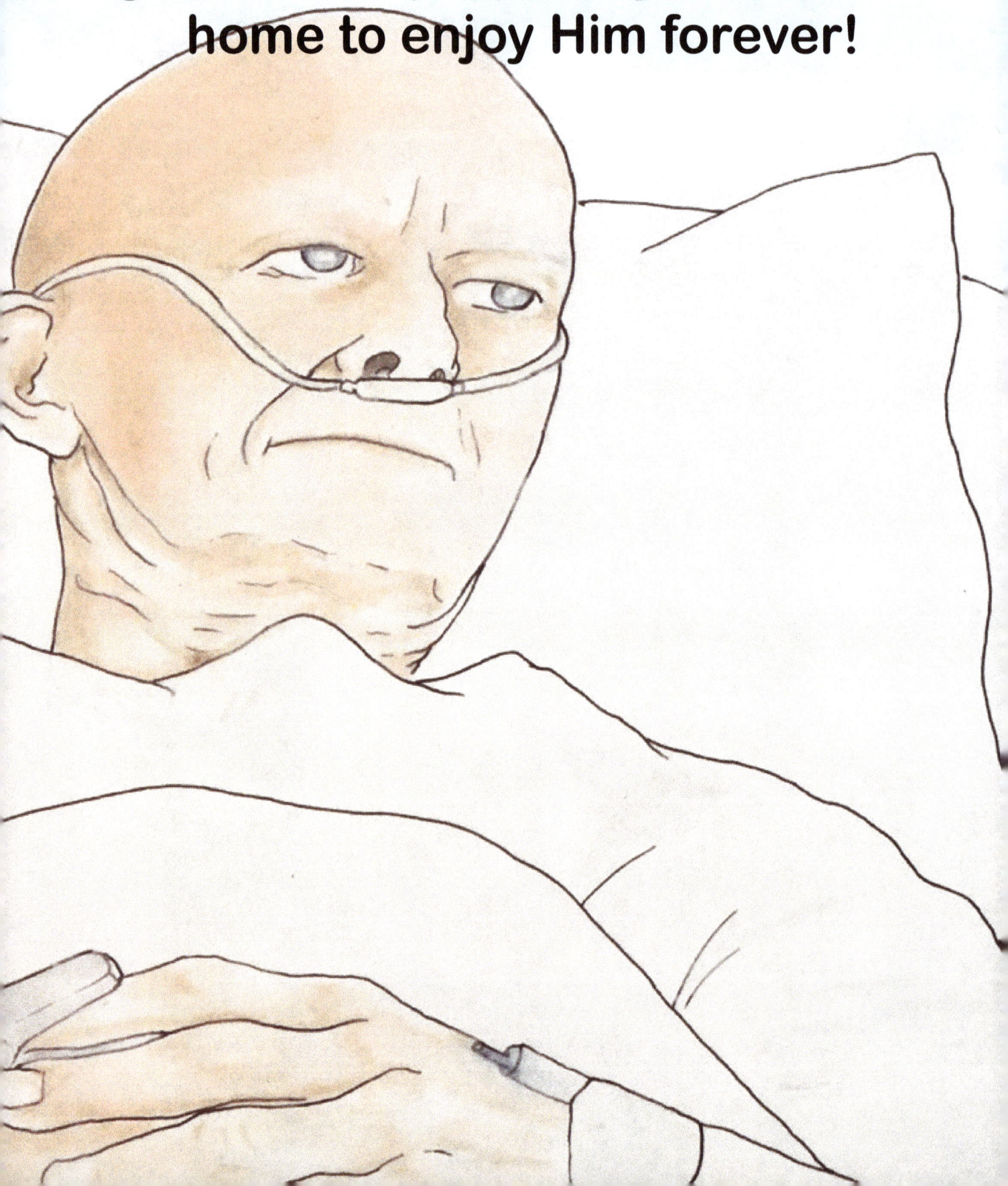

There truly is life beyond the bottle.

Another Bottle Please

Another drink I think

Just a few more sips on my lips

From the bottle like rain

Will wash away my pain

-Gene Baillie

As a deer pants for water,
so my soul pants for you, O God
my soul thirsts for God, for the living God.
When shall I come and appear before God?
My tears have been my food day and night,
while everyone says to me all the day long,
"Where is your God?"
O God, you are my God; earnestly I seek you;
my soul thirsts for you; my body faints for you,
like a dry and weary land with no water.
I sought You in the sanctuary,
to seek Your power and Your glory
Because Your steadfast love is better than life,
my lips will praise you.
Thus I will bless you as long as I live;
I will lift up my hands in your name
Psalms 42:1-3, 63:1-4 (author's translation)

Afterwords

Every book or work of art has a purpose, expressed, intended, or perceived by the author or artist—but does not necessarily match up with the recipient's impression while reading or viewing. This book provides words and art to provoke in you a review of why you are alive and for what purpose. The "art and message for life" is intended to be a conversation starter within yourself or with others concerning the direction of your life and its "end-game". It is no accident you have picked up this book, and no mistake you have read up to this point. If there is someone to talk with, start a conversation! Although the goal of this book is stated, it may not be what you saw as its purpose in your life. We encounter many bottles in life. Have you found any that satisfy your thirst or hunger? Any that solve any problems or difficulties? Maybe you realized none of the world's bottles satisfied or were a cure for any of a long list of your hopes, desires, disappointments, or even success moments. Maybe you need to ask beyond these bottles for Living Water that satisfies. If you have tasted Him who is good, then you also know you have a new "born date". The old is gone and you are a new creation.

Maybe you see yourself at some point or stage within this book. Maybe you are using various bottles to avoid the pain and disappointment you see in your life—you are trying to escape, deny, blame others for your situation, running away, considering suicide, have tried to overlook, tried to reconcile, tried negotiation or mediation, or even sought counsel or accountability. You may have also noticed that emptying any of the bottles was at best a temporary fix for the hunger or thirst representative of what you were experiencing. A bottle of water emptied to wash your hands will not keep them clean, nor satisfy your thirst. Nothing in yourself or from others has worked to give you peace, comfort, or a solution. You have been told you need to seek out the Lord and ask Him into your life. The only answer is that He is Lord and in control, not you. As you trust in Him, He will provide and sustain, even though the situation remains difficult and the storm still is a gale. He will not allow you to go through more than you can endure and will defend and preserve you. You need the Living Water of Jesus as your remedy, as written in John 4:10-14, *Jesus answered her (the woman living in sin), "If you knew the gift of God, and who it is that is saying to you, 'Give me a drink,' you would have asked him, and he would have given you living water." The woman said to him, "Sir, you have nothing to draw water with, and the well is deep. Where do you get that living water? Are you greater than our father Jacob? He gave us the well and drank from it himself, as did his sons and his livestock." Jesus said to her, "Everyone who drinks of this water will be thirsty again, but whoever drinks of the water that I will give him will never be thirsty again. The water that I will give him will become in him a spring of water welling up to eternal life."*

This message of 'Beyond the Bottle' is what the Lord intended and planned for you to read, and it either prompts you to also want eternal life beyond this life, or you already have this promise and certain hope. If you are reading this alone with no one else to talk with, and you do not know the Lord, please continue to read this section and then seek out Christian believers to discuss the message of God's mercy, remedy, and provision for His children. The first place to search is a pastor or leaders at a Christian church.

The Gospel message is simple and has been stated in many different ways. Here is one. God is Father, Son, and Holy Spirit. He created the universe including this world and everything in and upon it. He created man and man disobeyed God in the Garden of Eden. All mankind now is born in sin (spiritually dead), separated from God. Such a sinner has a bad heart, a bad record, and a bad life. According to God's perfect plan, you were born at the moment you were, and He has a purpose for every moment you are on this earth and beyond. There is not anything you can do to remedy the 3 problems of a bad heart, a bad record, and a bad life. By yourself, you cannot restore your relationship to God. But, God in His mercy and grace has a plan, a Savior, and His Spirit as the remedy and restoration. He chooses whom He will have follow Him. He causes His Holy Spirit to change your *heart* so you can understand and accept Jesus as your Lord and Savior. You see you have received the lasting treasure of His free gift of salvation. The sacrifice of Jesus provides His sinless *record* for yours, and you have the promise of eternal life through Him. He provides His Holy Spirit to guide and interpret His written truth of the Bible to every aspect of your life. You are a new creation, something we call new birth. You are an adopted child of God, a Christian. You now have an interest in seeking to live a holy and obedient *life* as you desire to read and study His Word, seek Christian fellowship, cast off worldly temptations, pray, seek to bear fruit as you grow where He plants you, as He provides for you, and gives you opportunities to share this good news with others.

Author Dr. Gene Baillie is a retired physician living in Anderson, SC. He grew up in rural Nebraska, the oldest of six children and the first member of his family to attend college. He and Gini were married for 51 years before her death in 2015 from the brain cancer, glioblastoma. Gene is father of 3 daughters and 4 foster sons, many grandchildren, and one great-grandson. He is an elder in the Presbyterian Church in America and author of four other books, all described and available at ReadGoodBooks.org. He encourages people to read and study the Bible. An 'Eternal Blueprint' gospel presentation (support for the 3 problems of a bad heart, record, and life) as well Bible study notes are available GeneBaillie@gmail.com

Illustrator Ty Davis is from Charleston, SC. During high school in Orangeburg, SC, his artistic talent blossomed and he and others realized his artistic abilities, his exhibiting skills and styles in painting, drawing, and sculpture, as well as music and fashion. Excelling and winning many awards, mastering figurative art (as rekindled in this book), he decided to change paths and set out to innovate the culture. Ty uses a technique where the paint is applied to the canvas and alcohol or water is used to let the composition "evolve". This creates a world relative to one's imagination and consciousness, a symphony far beyond the paintings, both confronting and comforting.
Contact Ty at tydavisbey@icloud.com

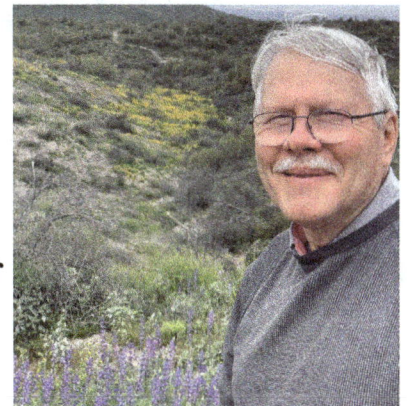

Record my misery;
list my tears on your scroll-
are they not in your record?
Then my enemies will turn back
when I call for help.
By this I will know that God is for me.
In God, whose word I praise,
in the Lord, whose word I praise—
in God I trust and am not afraid.
What can man do to me?
I am under vows to you, my God;
I will present my thank offerings to you.
For you have delivered me from death
and my feet from stumbling,
that I may walk before God
in the light of life.

Psalm 56: 8-13 (NIV)

Jesus guided me to
His Living Water
He will wipe away
every tear
Beyond the Bottle
He is!

Dr Gene Baillie
illustrated by Ty Davis
ReadGoodBooks.org
GeneBaillie@gmail.com

Beyond the Bottle, the Abstract Story

After the book was ready to print, Dr. Baillie commissioned Ty to use his current passion and talent of unique abstract art ability to envision what this book and its message would look like in his abstract environment. He was again given complete freedom to express utilizing his paint and alcohol evolution techniques. Although most abstract artists intend for the viewer to independently interpret what they see, many of us, including Dr. Baillie, have difficulty seeing and perceiving the extensive message of abstract art. So, Ty provided a description of what was originally and ongoing in his mind and heart to express the intense message of *Beyond the Bottle*.

"This is a story about a journey or simply a return to the everlasting love and forgiveness of the Lord, which is my interpretation of *Beyond the Bottle*. Going from right to left, starting on the bottom, the return starts (note the black figure several places along the bottom). Moving across the path of life we encounter and must pass through a vast valley (or desert). On the left, you see this leads us to a staircase with broken stones at the base. This staircase leads to nowhere, and below is the black area of desolation and destruction. When lifted from the pit, above we see the golden staircase (example of Jesus as the way, the truth and the life), and we see we are united with Christ on the blue pathway depicted upward to the right. In the upper right are round objects that are the sun and moon, and the 3rd suggesting an eye. This indicates the heavenly. Additionally the 3 objects are a face that is above the area suggesting mountains (His holy hill).

Throughout the story there is 'abstract writing' starting with 'Thou art holy' in the right bottom. Hidden in the blackness of the lower left is 'Abide in My love'. In the top left corner is "77 times" from Matthew 18:22 concerning forgiveness. The words 'great work' are in the valley. 'Abide in my love' is again repeated in the upper right, highlighting the work of forgiveness and ceaseless love of our Lord.

Multiple layers of red, yellow and a little bit of blue were used for this painting. Primary colors of red, blue and yellow were chosen to excite and move the eyes. The paint is mixed with alcohol, so as it dries, it evolves with imperceptible merging. So, after a layer of ink dries, layers are added, using inks depending on the color needed. In this work, yellow and blue could not be used at the same time because it would merge before drying and make green. Blue, minimally merged with red gives hints of purple, and a mix of all the colors gives the hopelessness of black."

This description helped Dr. Baillie understand how we do indeed synthesize black on white to easily see and read text, but this concept of synthesizing colors with blending or merging of colors is so important to lead us to see and perceive what is in an image, using many, if not all our senses—far beyond the black and white, more factual presentations. This is an amazing process for me as I am understanding more about the abstract processes within myself. It is amazing grace. I am truly like the blind man in John 9, "I once was blind and now I see!" I too have eyes to see, but was not "seeing" until helped.

As you view this art, again and again, with or without reading this description, you will have a multitude of other thoughts and interpretations of what you see, a whole range of constantly changing views and viewpoints.

After completing this book, I come to this work with some bias. But it is also comforting to break away from my perception that abstract art was vague at best. I felt if we did not know what the artist intended, we are seemingly hopeless to have a clue as to any proper message or interpretation. So, now the following are some of my newly acquired observations and interpretations.

Did you see the vague blue 'figure' lower left (suggesting to me Jesus lifting us from the miry pit)? Also, the many crosses cause my eye movement and focus, I see the first golden cross right lower to be representative of a cross almost everyone knows exists and its meaning, but they are divided into two groups, the ones that love and understand the meaning of the cross related to their earthly and eternal lives, and the others who hate the cross and everything it stands for, disbelieving it all—they do not have eyes to see or ears to hear. There are 2 more crosses in the lower right amongst the seeming jumbled letters. These crosses are missed unless you are really looking. They are part of the abstract words, 'Thou art holy'. The cross that is the letter *T* of Thou is not obvious at first, but then you realize it almost has hands outstretched, while others see it as a pitchfork symbol. Another cross is located beside the word work, to again remind you God is at work as you go through the valleys in your life (instead of thinking you having to work for His favor), and another cross is subtly included in the letter *t* of great. The final cross is above the black pit of destruction and despair. Those lifted up recognize it is on its side, as it has served its intended purpose. You know it now represents the empty cross. You begin your trek on the blue line which seems to represent the King's Highway, joining the others (notice the linear blue streaks with white spherical centers that suggest fish to some, as you remember the fish is used as a Christian symbol).